Praise for *embrace you*

"Do you remember a beautiful place in nature where you felt inspired, at peace, and filled with wonder? In *Embrace Your Inner Wild*, author Mary Reynolds Thompson and photographer Don Moseman interweave stunning images and stirring words that capture our imagination. This book reminds us that our journey on Earth has been alongside animals, and that each of us is connected to the wild places. This is a book that you will want to return to again and again to refresh the glimpse of splendor found within its pages."

Catriona MacGregor, Vision & Nature Quest Leader and author of the award winning book
Partnering with Nature: The Wild Path to Reconnecting with the Earth

"Each turn of the page brings stunning prose poems and breathtaking images. Mary Reynolds Thompson's connection to her own 'inner wild' is transparent as sunrise, brazen as a bullfinch, and soul-stirringly, achingly gorgeous."

Kathleen Adams, Director, Center for Journal Therapy, and author of the bestselling
Journal to the Self: Twenty-Two Paths to Personal Growth

"My heart smiles in wonder and delight as I turn each page. The photographs are amazing, and the reflections guide me to that numinous place which is, simultaneously, within and without."

Elizabeth Ayres, author of Invitation to Wonder: A Journey through the Seasons
and Founder of the Center for Creative Writing

"Only someone with Don Moseman's patience to walk across continents could hold a camera for hours on a bobcat that itself is holding its position for hours during a hunt. The resulting images of animals behaving as if nobody were watching are deeply affecting and show wildness in its truest sense. For many, the images and accompanying text by Mary Reynolds Thompson will impel both celebration and protection in equal measure."

Jim Kravets, Founder and former editor, West Marin Citizen *Newspaper*

embrace your inner wild

52 Reflections for an Eco-Centric World

Don Moseman

May R. Thompson

Mary Reynolds Thompson with photographs by Don Moseman

White Cloud Press
Ashland, Oregon

White Cloud Press, PO Box 3400, Ashland, OR 97520
www.whitecloudpress.com

Printed in China

First printed in 2011

Library of Congress Cataloging-in-Publication Data
Thompson, Mary Reynolds, 1956-
Embrace your inner wild : 52 reflections for an eco-centric world / by Mary Reynolds Thompson with photographs by Don Moseman.
    p. cm.
 ISBN 978-1-935952-53-4 (pbk.)
1. Wildlife photography. 2. Nature--Anecdotes. I. Moseman, Don. II. Title.
 TR729.W54T565 2011
 779'.32--dc23
                              2011025909

introduction

In wildness is the preservation of the world. HENRY DAVID THOREAU

This book invites you to embrace your Inner Wild—a place within you of pure aliveness.

In our high-tech, high-stress, overbuilt world, embracing our Inner Wild is more essential than ever. Modernity can be deadening—to the planet and to our own souls. But thankfully, if we look for it, wildness still abounds.

The fiercely intelligent eyes of the coyote; the sharp, scything wings of the white-tailed kite; the way light trembles on water—all elicit a deep response. In our encounters with nature we come to realize that we, too, are part of the windswept forests and the rain-fed rivers. We see nothing strange in talking to trees or feeling our spirits soar to the spiraling of hawks.

Embracing our Inner Wild, we awaken to wonder. And to oneness.

Don Moseman and I have crossed paths many times on the trails of Marin County, California, where we live. While we commune with nature through different means—Don carries his camera, and I, my journal—our roots reach into the same earth. We are both working to preserve wildness, wherever it resides—within and without.

From that shared passion this book was born.

escape

The cage door isn't locked.
We can open it at any time, let our souls rise, wide-winged, wild.
Ask the osprey, the hawk, the way to live and be free.

longing

Trees shimmer, crows caw, the distance beckons

Like the wind, my heart longs to travel across the land, touch each perfect thing.

Dragonflies dart through the early morning air.

Red ones like hot chili. Blue ones bright as sapphires.

Brown ones, green ones, with wingspans wide as my hand.

The day has barely begun, and already so many miracles.

morning magic

turning point

The geese promenade, making their
stately way to the other side of the pond.
A sudden shift. They turn as one,
forming a perfect V. The movement
of a moment. Wings thunder the air.
Voices rise like revving engines.
And they're gone. If only we, as one,
could change directions as quickly.

bully

You should never have been introduced. You don't belong. You cause a lot of damage in the neighborhood. Salamander, steelhead, and red-legged frogs, even birds, aren't safe from your wicked appetites—better for all if you were gone.

But as I look at you in your springy green suit, it's hard not to be taken in.

You're a bad boy Bullfrog, but still you make my heart leap.

No phones, no Internet, no TV, no Blackberries,
no iPods, no distractions.

No telling what marvelous things could happen
with so much space and time and silence to fill.

unplugged

The white-tailed kite lifts
into the cloudless sky
and hovers for hours—
pure light, pure spirit—
nothing to weigh her
down. From her,
we learn how to live
more lightly.

lightness of being

wild cat

A woman came into the vet's office carrying what she referred to as a large tabby cat. She had found him by the side of the road, alive but unconscious. She placed him in the backseat of her car and drove the twenty minutes to the vet.

"Just as well the cat didn't wake up," the vet told me later. "He was a bobcat. Would have torn that woman and her car to bits." Reason enough, I think, to give the wild in us plenty of space to roam and play.

memory

Whoosh, whoosh, whoosh.

A raven flies overhead and I flash back to a stormy
day in childhood, curtains flapping like pinions.

They say fragrance is the portal to memory, but some
days childhood returns, carried on the wings of sound.

contentment

A goldfinch swoops by with a tiny seed in his beak. He sits on a branch in the sun looking for all the world like happiness. For days I have done nothing but hike, sleep, and eat. Each day, the wildflowers, the sky, and the light seem more wonderful. Each day, I am brought closer to the true nature of joy.

Learn to sing the river's song,
root yourself in tree wisdom,
study the syntax of stone.
As you enter the wild,
learn its language.
To listen to a raindrop,
or a raven, or a rock
is to reclaim part of your
own untold story.

river song

Water covers 70 percent
of the Earth and comprises
70 percent of our bodies.
A miraculous inheritance,
like looking into the
mirror and seeing your
mother's eyes.

inheritance

transformation

I dream of snakes. Giant cobras with collars of glittering blue stones, snakes writhing in golden meadows, or slipping under rocks into dark caverns. At home, I watch gopher snakes, king snakes, and the occasional rattler glide across my path.

Yet what fascinates me most about snakes is this: before they shed their skins, their eyes—covered in scales—turn a dull, bluish white so they cannot see clearly. I'm reminded of blind faith, the courage to let go of what no longer serves us, even when we don't have a clear vision of the future.

Letting go isn't easy. But imagine the moment when the scales fall from the eyes—is it possible that the world has never looked so beautiful?

You could always drive to the top, but walking, you might
discover the wild strength of the mountain lives within you.

The air cools for a moment, turns dark.

You spot the vulture directly overhead. Red of face,
dower of dress, inky wings shimmer like black silk.

Death settles in like this. At first dimly perceived.
Then full-bodied. Strong-winged. Astonishingly graceful.

foreshadowing

Head tucked, eyes
steady, feathers still,
the night heron stands
in the water waiting
for a fish to swim by.

Everything you
need to know about
concentration has just
been shown to you.

hard times

Surrounded by concrete, steel, plastic, our hearts grow hard.
It's time to lie down in the long grass and touch the soft Earth again.

not gone

When my friend Elizabeth died
she promised she would try
to stay near to us in nature for
as long as she could.

Now a hummingbird
visits me on my walks,
hovers at eye level.

Unmistakably still here.

It's only March, but it's hit 93 degrees for ten days in a row. I walk the hills in a haze of heat. Wild irises bend in brown grasses, riverbeds crack like calloused knuckles, and birds sit dazed on frazzled branches. The small signs hold the larger story.

The crickets sing of a dry land.

fevered spring

wetland poem

Gray and blue grasses. Flights across the moon.
At night, a smooth sheet of paper written on by stars.

Black shiny nose, bushy tail shaped like a pinecone. Coyote. Ears cocked, tawny pelt camouflaged by rattlesnake grass. Every part of me awake now—no coffee necessary. I savor this long, strong sip of wildness.

morning visitor

stung A yellow jacket stings me twice. I lift my shirt, curse. Some say it's reason enough to stay away from the wild —these things that claw, bite, burn. But couldn't you say the same about love? And who would choose to live without that?

hide and seek

Shhh. . . . Don't make a sound. Wait patiently. Your wild soul has a shy side. Approach it as you would any wild animal —quietly, unnoticed. Only then will it reveal itself to you.

running on empty

When we're low on energy and inner resources, it's easy to snap. Get mad. So why do we think we can burn through the Earth's resources without her losing her cool?

A boy disappears into the woods every day and doesn't return for hours.

"Why do you spend so much time there?" his father asks.

"Because it's where I go to find God," the boy answers.

"Haven't I taught you that God's the same everywhere?"

"Yes," the boy replies, "but I'm not."

woodland story

listen

Away from the hum, roar, rev, and clatter of
modern life, you will discover a space so
silent you can hear the whisper of your soul.

stop for awe

An old man stops his truck beside me on the dusty path, unwinds his window, leans out and points one bony finger to the sky. "Contrails," he tells me, his voice quavering with excitement as we stare at the white streaks of condensation from the passing plane.

Strange guy. But not nearly as strange as those who never take the time to be amazed.

What happens when the charismatic creatures of our childhood are gone? When the polar bear, tiger, and gray wolf of storybooks no longer walk the Earth? Does our love of a particular animal fade just because it's extinct? Or are we left with a sense of emptiness, a feeling of being in some way incomplete?

birdflowers

Beaks blossom from the bark of trees.

And tiny starlings become for an instant, birdflowers.

For the untamed, life is wondrous.

meadow wisdom

A sheet unfurled beneath a burnished sky, grass and light stretch off into the distance, touching eternity.

Is it possible that in wide-open spaces our souls grow larger?

If the bees vanish, life on this
planet as we know it will end.

Fewer plants, fewer fruits, less beauty.

So much hinges on the smallest things.

small is beautiful

The first glad shout of water hollers down the riverbed,

as if to say, "Okay, the dry spell is over—let's go!"

Move softly, glance sideways,
watch for the slightest movement.
Rely on something deeper than
thought to guide you on your path,
like the deer in the forest.

instinct

plumage

Slender feet raised in slow succession, a snowy egret walks by— elegant as Nefertiti. And almost made extinct, simply because women once wanted feathers in their hats.

Better, perhaps, to be less well dressed, that Earth remain adorned.

A mother seal caresses, nuzzles
her pup, to recognize him as her
own. An ancient ritual in which
she comes to bond with her child.

As we, too, activate our love for
the Earth by touching, tending,
placing our hands on her mottled,
brown body.

In loving, we come to love.

staying in touch

singing the world alive

For 50 million years songbirds have sung the day alive. But as forests are felled and meadows paved, as city lights confuse night flyers, these birds are fast disappearing. Almost half lost in the last forty years. And all I can think is:

Who will sing the world alive now?

The deeper we go
into our individual
nature, the more we
discover that we are
part of the whole.

paradox

Take the egret that fans its feathers, lifts its thin legs, prances up and down, a ballerina of the marshlands. As you, too, leave behind your everyday identity and become writer, dreamer, painter, poet. . . .

night vision

In the shadow, nourishment waits for you. Go into the dark with bright eyes.

Wildflowers cling where they can. Their colors ripen and rejoice, gathering bees, hummingbirds, and butterflies.

Yet how carelessly we pave over them—these precious teachers of how to grow wild, beautiful, free.

gathering place

oceans of beauty

The most radiant being I ever saw was the ocean
with the sun full upon it. Like a beautiful lady at
a ball, her sequined skirts moved to the music
of the tides and winds. And watching her dance,
I thought, when I grow up, this is how I want to be.

living on the edge

Civilized and citified, in the depth of our souls there remains
a deep need to experience nature's drama and danger.

circling

A red-tailed hawk spins and loops—tail, canyonland red.

And I, who began my walk filled
with urgency and deadlines,

gaze upwards, becoming sky,
becoming cloud, becoming air.

A friend asks an indigenous elder from the rain forests of South America, "Are you ever lonely?"

Silence.

"There is no word for loneliness in his language," the translator explains.

unlearning loneliness

here and now

Only in the present moment can you take the next step.

wild air

Forests are the lungs of the planet, the breath of language and of song. In them, we breathe more easily. Yet today, 70 percent of the world's original forests are gone; 95 percent of old-growth forests in North America are gone; two-thirds of Earth's tropical rain forests are gone.

So shocking, it takes my breath away.

What if we discovered
we are happiest outdoors,
miles from the cities,
towns, and technologies
we spend so much time
and effort creating? What
if we simply stopped
pouring our energy into
more of the same?

What if we reached
instead for the whole
world, and the stars too?
What if we walked away
from anything that did
not bring us alive?

what if?

disturbances in the field

A large bobcat turned and locked his yellow eyes on mine.

Days after, it was as if every nerve, sinew,
tawny hair of his body now pulsed in me.

No longer an abstraction, but wildness absorbed.

Can you sense how the whole of creation is altered by your presence?

Take one step into the woods and listen.

impact

When we age, our bones become
more porous, lighter—like those of a bird.
Are we, too, readying ourselves for flight?

flight

You enter a forest as a storm hits. Trunks and branches sway in a wild, rustling dance. Yet the trees remain standing, rooted firmly to the ground.

Imagine that you are so rooted in your own true nature that no storm could topple you. How would it be to live your life from that place?

rooted in
the earth

moontalk

Watching the moon grow from a tiny cup into a circular bowl,

you see how life progresses toward wholeness.

The moon enters the next phase of its existence—now you must look for yours.

Mary's Story

One blustery December weekend in 1983, I was hiking the Marin Headlands above the Pacific Ocean. I'd quit drinking a few days earlier. The storming surf mirrored my inner turmoil. And yet, the wildness of the waves calmed me.

I tasted salt and didn't know if it was the ocean's or mine. I felt completely at one with that deep body of water.

Since then, the natural world has been my guide, helping me to discover my own Inner Wild.

Born and raised in London, England, I've trekked all over the planet, from the Himalayas to the Andes. But it's the golden hills of Marin County that I now call home. I walk the trails daily with my husband, Bruce, who shares my love for the natural world and the wild soul that unites us all.

Language, not nature, was my first love. In my early forties, I left my career as a copywriter and branding expert to become a facilitator of poetry and journal therapy—and my focus shifted. The raw poetry of the natural world connected me to my interior world. Every walk became a revelation—a doorway to my Inner Wild.

This book is part of that continuing journey. It is also an example of a unique program of ecological spirituality. To learn more about my work, please visit my website: www.reclaimingthewildsoul.com

Don's Story,
a.k.a., "Walkin' Don"

I'd look out at Mount Tamalpais through the bars of San Quentin State Prison and promise myself I'd walk to the top when I got out. I did. And somehow I never stopped walking. I crossed America on foot three times, earning the nickname "Walkin' Don."

The wild is my lifeline. It's how I connect with my deeper nature. It helps me walk through life sober and serene. And free.

In 2005, I took up photography and found a new way to commune with the wild. It requires patience to track down an elusive bobcat or wait for the annual return of the ospreys to their nests. But thirty years in prison, if nothing else, teaches you patience.

Today I show my photos at the Raptor Center at Fort Cronkhite, and at schools throughout the Bay Area. I also talk to prison inmates, sharing my story and showing them what freedom can really mean.

Most often, you'll find me close to the Earth, walking the trails of Marin County, in search of the next wild encounter, the next "perfect" shot.

To view more of my photographs, visit me on Facebook:https://www.facebook.com/#!/walkindon

Appendix

COVER
Coyote,
Bolinas Ridge
Fire Road,
West Marin

PAGE 4
Racoon,
backyard,
San Rafael

PAGES 10-11
**Black-tailed
buck,** taken
from Mount
Tamalpais

PAGE 2
Muskrat,
Bolinas Marsh

PAGE 5
**Black-tailed
fawns;** Kent
Lake, Marin
Municipal
Water District

PAGES 12-13
**Meadowhawk
Dragonfly,** Lake
Lagunitas, Marin
Municipal Water
District

PAGE 2
Snowy Egrets,
Las Gallinas
Salt Ponds,
San Rafael

PAGE 5
**Honeybee and
Black-chinned
Hummingbird,**
Fort Cronkhite,
Golden Gate
National Rec-
reational Area

PAGES 14-15
Canada Goose,
Las Gallinas
Salt Ponds,
San Rafael

PAGE 3
Bobcat, Bobcat
Trail, Fort
Cronkhite, Golden
Gate National
Recreational Area

PAGES 6-7
**Western
Bluebird,**
Las Gallinas Salt
Ponds, San
Rafael

PAGES 16-17
Bullfrog, Lake
Lagunitas, Marin
Municipal Water
District

PAGE 3
**Allen's Humming-
bird,** Coastal Trail,
Fort Cronkhite,
Golden Gate
National Recre-
ational Area

PAGE 8
**Juvenile
Red-tailed
Hawk,** Tomales
Bay, Point
Reyes National
Seashore

PAGES 18-19
**Northern River
Otter,** Las Gallina
Salt Ponds, San
Rafael

PAGE 4
**Female and
male fledgling
Barn Owls,** San
Pedro Mountain,
San Rafael

PAGE 9
Osprey, Bon
Tempe Lake,
Marin Municipal
Water District

PAGES 20-21
**White-tailed
Kite,** above
Bolinas
Lagoon,
Golden Gate
National Parks
Conservancy

 PAGES 22-23
Bobcat,
Haypress Camp
Trail, Tennessee
Valley

 PAGES 32-33
Garter Snake,
Smith Fire Road,
Loma Alta Open
Space Preserve,
Fairfax

 PAGE 41
**Sara Orange-tip
butterfly**, Kent
Pump Fire Road,
Marin Municipal
Water District

 PAGE 24
American Crows,
Marin County

 PAGES 34-35
**Mount
Tamalpais**,
looking east

 PAGE 41
**Black-tailed
fawns**; Kent
Lake, Marin
Municipal
Water District

 PAGE 25
Common Raven,
Marin County

 PAGES 36-37
Turkey Vultures,
Pierce Point
Road, Point
Reyes National
Seashore

 PAGES 42-43
**Allen's Humming-
bird**, Coastal Trail,
Fort Cronkhite,
Golden Gate
National Recre-
ational Area

 PAGES 26-27
**American
Goldfinch**,
Lake Lagunitas,
Marin Municipal
Water District

 PAGES 38-39
**Black-crowned
Night-Heron**,
Bolinas Lagoon,
Golden Gate
National Parks
Conservancy

 PAGES 44-45
**Red-tailed
Hawk**, Sir
Francis Drake
Boulevard, Point
Reyes National
Seashore

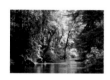 PAGES 28-29
**Lagunitas
Creek**, Samuel
P. Taylor State
Park

 PAGE 40
**Monarch
butterfly**, Bolinas
Ridge Fire Road,
West Marin

 PAGE 46
Bolinas Lagoon,
Golden Gate
National Parks
Conservancy

 PAGES 30-31
Great Egret,
Las Gallinas Salt
Ponds, San
Rafael

 PAGE 41
House Finch,
Bolinas Park,
Fairfax

 PAGE 47
Great Blue Heron,
Muir Beach

Appendix

PAGE 47
Lake Lagunitas,
Marin Municipal
Water District

PAGE 47
**Great Blue
Heron**, Lake
Lagunitas

PAGE 47
**Snowy Egrets
and American
Avocets**,
Las Gallinas
Salt Ponds,
San Rafael

PAGES 48-49
Coyote, Bolinas
Ridge Fire Road,
West Marin

PAGES 50-51
Yellow jacket,
Tarmac Road,
Marin County

PAGE 52
Brush rabbit,
Tennessee Valley
trail, Marin
Headlands

PAGE 53
Muskrat, San
Rafael Water
Treatment Pond,
off Francisco
Boulevard

PAGE 53
**Orange-crowned
Warbler**, Bobcat
Trail, Fort
Cronkhite Golden
Gate National
Recreational Area

PAGE 53
Chipmunk, Muir
Woods National
Monument

PAGES 54-55
**Juvenile
Red-tailed Hawk**,
off Pierce Ranch
Road, Point Reyes
National Seashore

PAGES 56-57
Chipmunk, Muir
Woods National
Monument

PAGE 58
Tomales Bay,
Point Reyes
National
Seashore

PAGE 59
**Fledging
Red-shouldered
Hawk**,
off Lucas Valley
Road, Terra Linda

PAGE 60
Northern Flicker,
Ponti Fire Road,
San Rafael

PAGE 61
California Quail,
Pacheco Valley,
Novato

PAGE 61
Wild Turkey,
Lucas Valley
Road, Terra
Linda

PAGES 62-63
**Juvenile Northern
Harrier**, looking
toward China
Camp State Park,
San Rafael

PAGES 64-65
European Starlin
off Highway 1 nea
Marshall, Point Re
National Seashore

PAGES 66-67
Rodeo Valley,
Southern Marin

PAGES 74-75
Snowy Egret,
Bolinas Lagoon,
Golden Gate
National Parks
Conservancy

PAGE 86
**Northern
Checkerspot
butterfly**, Marin
County

PAGE 68
Sweet Peas,
Marin County

PAGES 76-77
Harbor seals,
Bolinas Lagoon,
Golden Gate
National Parks
Conservancy

PAGE 87
**Allen's Humming-
bird** on Twinberry
bush

Page 69
**Bumble Bee and
Lupine**, Dipsea
Trail, Stinson
Beach

PAGES-78-79
Song Sparrow,
Matt Davis Trail,
Mount Tamalpais
State Park

PAGES 88-89
Bodega Bay,
just north of
Marin County

PAGE 70
Calla lily pod

PAGES 80-81
**Orb weaver
spider**,
Muir Woods
National
Monument

PAGES 90-91
Osprey nest,
above Kent Lake,
Marin Municipal
Water District

PAGE 71
Fern Creek Trail,
Mount Tamalpais
State Park

PAGES 82-83
Snowy Egret,
Bolinas Lagoon,
Golden Gate
National Parks
Conservancy

PAGES 92-93
Red-tailed Hawk,
Pantoll Trailhead,
Mount Tamalpais
State Park

PAGES 72-73
**Black-tailed
Doe**, Sky Oaks,
Marin Municipal
Water District

PAGES 84-85
Burrowing Owl,
Bobcat Trail above
Tennessee Valley

PAGES 94-95
**Female and male
fledgling Barn
Owls**, San Pedro
Mountain, San
Rafael

Appendix

PAGES 96-97
**Great Blue
Heron**, Lake
Lagunitas, Marin
Municipal Water
District

PAGES 106-107
Snowy Egrets,
Las Gallinas
Salt Ponds,
San Rafael

PAGE 119
**Black-chinned
Hummingbird and
chicks**, Lucas Valle
Road, Terra Linda

PAGES 98-99
**Red-shouldered
Hawk**, Tomales
Bay, Point Reyes
National
Seashore

PAGES 108-109
American Kestrel,
Female, perched
on Douglas Fir
above Panoramic,
Mount Tamalpais
State Park

PAGE 125
**Golden-crowned
Sparrow**, Mount
Tamalpais State
Park

PAGES 100-101
Gray squirrel,
China Camp
State Park,
San Rafael

PAGES 110-111
**Moon over
Marin County**

PAGES 127
**Western
Bluebirds**,
Sky Trail, Point
Reyes National
Seashore

PAGES 102-103
Bobcat, Bobcat
Trail, Fort
Cronkhite, Golden
Gate National
Recreational Area

PAGE 112
**Feet of Great
Blue Heron**,
Las Gallinas
Salt Ponds,
San Rafael

PAGES 128
Gadwell duck,
Las Gallinas Salt
Ponds,
San Rafael

PAGE 104
**Pacific-slope
Flycatcher**,
Mount Tamalpais
State Park

PAGE 113
**Great Horned
Owl chicks**,
Lucas Valley
Road, Terra
Linda

BACK COVER
American Kestrel,
Pierce Ranch
Road, Point Reyes
National Seashore

PAGE 105
Wilson Warbler,
Sky Trail, Point
Reyes National
Seashore

PAGE 118
Driftwood,
Tomales Bay,
Point Reyes
National Seashore

Acknowledgements

The wild thrives on diverse community and so do books.

From Mary:
My deep gratitude goes to my friend and mentor, Kay Adams, of the Center for Journal Therapy. Her gifted work with the healing power of language continues to guide my path.

To my Hummingbird sisters, Annie Robinson, Lee Doyle, and Julia McNeal, my heartfelt thanks. Your brilliant insights and editing are so much a part of this book. Elizabeth Banning, I feel your joyful presence hovering about us.

I am forever grateful to my beloved friend Rachel de Baere. She invited me into her writing circle and then into the International Women's Writing Guild, and life was never the same.

Marilyn Steele, Wendy Wallbridge, Richelle McClain, Jacquelyn Wells, Heidi Lyss, Jeffrey Erkelens, and William Carney have my enduring thanks and friendship for their love and support over the many years of walking the writing path together.

To Kathy Kuser, thank you! Our wild and sacred friendship continues to inspire my work.

To my darling husband, Bruce, you are the joy of my wild soul. With your love and support, everything is possible.

Don thanks his contributor and good colleague, Rickey Hendricks, Ph.D., as well as his mentor, Stuart Schwartz of The Image Flow.

Together, we thank Brooke Warner for her belief in us and her help in finding our amazing publisher, Steve Scholl. The extraordinarily talented Kari Ontko is responsible for the stunning design of this book. It was her dramatic vision that brought the words and images together. Allen

Fish, Director of the Golden Gate Raptor Observatory, was an invaluable source of information about raptors and other feathered beings.

Most of all, we thank those who fight to protect wildness everywhere. Wild creatures and places fill our souls and remind us of how beautiful and extraordinary life is.

For the love of the Earth, its inhabitants, and the wild soul that longs to be set free.

Please share your wild encounters with us at
www.embraceyourinnerwild.com